KELLER:
KLEIDER MACHEN LEUTE

by

B. A. ROWLEY
Lecturer in German
University College, London

EDWARD ARNOLD (PUBLISHERS) LTD.
41 Maddox Street, London W.1

Printed in Great Britain by
Butler & Tanner Ltd., Frome and London

Preface

In arranging the material for my six chapters, I have deliberately avoided the unreal dichotomy of form and content,
although there is a progressive shift of emphasis from one
aspect to the other. The sources of the story are included in
Chapter 6, partly for the light they throw on the problem of
'poetry and truth' in Keller, and partly to remove an unnec-
essary screen between reader and literary text. References to
secondary sources are given in full only where details of the
source do not appear in the 'Select Bibliography'.

The latter indicates my debt to Keller criticism only very
partially, my debt to literary theory not at all. I am glad to
record my thanks to the many students with whom I have
discussed this and other stories by Keller; one of them, Miss
P. M. Craven, has been kind enough to read and comment
on the manuscript. Dr. J. C. Middleton and Dr. G. T. Hughes
provided bibliographical information, and Dr. Hughes ar-
ranged for the loan of some important items which are difficult of access. I have learned much from discussing Keller
with him over the years, as also from Mr. T. D. Jones and
from the late Mr. E. K. Bennett, who did so much to en-
courage English interest in German literature of the nine-
teenth century. My colleagues at University College, Mrs.
W. Nowottny, Mr. D. G. Mowatt, Professor L.W. Forster
and Mrs. Forster, and especially Miss E. M. Wilkinson, have
read all or part of the manuscript and made invaluable sug-
gestions, as well as helping me in more general ways. Finally,
I should like to thank my wife for her constructive criticism
and constant understanding.

B. A. R.

LONDON
Whit Monday 1959

Contents

1. Genesis and Publication

Kleider machen Leute has established itself as one of the best and most popular of Keller's stories. This has been the opinion, not of literary critics only, but of the general reader, to judge from the number of times it has been reprinted—in England, France, Sweden, America and South Africa, as well as in the German-speaking countries. Moreover, it has been translated into French (1873, 1933), English (1876, 1884–8, 1891, 1929), Norwegian (1916), Danish (1919), Spanish (1922–3), Italian (1932) and Welsh (1948); and it provided Alexander Zemlinsky with the basis for his comic opera of the same title, performed in Vienna in 1910, and published in Vienna and New York, 1922.

It first appeared, as the opening story of the second series of *Die Leute von Seldwyla*, in December 1873; the date on the title-page, however, is 1874. The first Seldwyla stories had appeared long before, in 1856. Keller intended to follow this first cycle with another almost immediately, and indeed he had a contract with his publisher, Friedrich Vieweg, in Brunswick, to deliver the new manuscript by 1 April 1857. Political disturbances in Switzerland, and the distraction of Keller's other projects and activities, however, hampered its completion, and it was not until February 1860 that the first of the new stories, *Die missbrauchten Liebesbriefe*, was sent off. Further delay was occasioned by Keller's appointment to the important post of Clerk to the Canton of Zürich in the autumn of 1861, and the next story, *Der Schmied seines Glückes*, followed only in

June 1865. By 1872 the series was at last nearing completion;
but then a disagreement over the terms on which the first
series was to be reprinted led to the cancellation of the contract,
in March 1873. A new one was made, almost at once, with the
Stuttgart firm of G. J. Göschen; and the manuscript was now
rapidly completed.

Because of the length of time during which Keller was thus
engaged on the collection, we do not know exactly when
Kleider machen Leute was conceived or written. It was probably
completed by mid–1871, when Keller wrote to Vieweg on
25 July: 'Ich rücke endlich allmählig dem Abschlusse des
zweiten Bandes der Leute von Seldwyla entgegen', and
mentions 'die noch hier liegenden Manuskripte'. This must
refer to *Kleider machen Leute*, since two stories were already in
Vieweg's hands, and the two others were still unfinished
eighteen months later, as Keller admits to Vieweg on 13
December 1872. In this letter Keller refers to *Kleider machen
Leute* by name for the first time, and describes it as 'ready'.

At the other end, the story was almost certainly not conceived, in its present form, before 1857, since there is no
mention of it in the notes for the second series which Keller
jotted down in that year. Jakob Bächtold, Keller's first
biographer, dates it 'at the beginning of the 1860's', without
offering any evidence, and this lead is followed by Ermatinger
and by Boeschenstein, who bases his view on resemblances he
perceives to *Das Fähnlein der sieben Aufrechten*, written in
1860. More recent opinion, however (notably Wüst, Fränkel,
Rothbarth and Ermatinger himself writing in 1926), favours
a later date: not before 1863, and possibly towards the end of
the 1860's. A number of factors make this later date probable.

The *Novelle* includes important material drawn from Keller's contacts with Polish patriots during the Revolution of 1863/64. Jakob Frey's story *Das erfüllte Versprechen* (1862) may have provided Keller with the impetus to write. The manuscript, which was bought back after the death of the publisher and is now in the Keller *Nachlass*, is written on the folio-sized paper used by Keller for his official reports, and thus available only from 1861 onwards. And finally: if the story had been completed earlier, it would almost certainly have been sent off to Vieweg in fulfilment of Keller's obligations. The best estimate we can make, therefore, is that it was written between 1864 and 1871, perhaps after the completion of *Der Schmied seines Glückes* in 1865, and probably over a period of several years.

And yet, some of the material for it was present in the author's mind long before. As we shall see, the story derives in part from an incident which took place in Wädenswyl about the year 1844, and which probably came to Keller's attention soon afterwards. In a sense, therefore, *Kleider machen Leute* took some twenty-five years to crystallize in Keller's mind.

2. Structure

An edition of *Kleider machen Leute* by Fadrus and Obendorfer (Vienna, 1956) divides the text into sections headed 'Auf der Walz', 'Im Gasthof "Zur Waage" ', ' "Graf" Strapinski', 'Gast auf dem Gut des Amtsrates', etc. Had Keller wanted to divide his story, he would no doubt have done so. In fact, there

are no typographical indications of structure whatever[1]—
neither 'chapters' marked by printer's rules, as in *Romeo und
Julia auf dem Dorfe*, nor structurally conceived paragraphs, as in
Kleist's story *Das Erdbeben in Chili.*—Wolfgang Kayser, indeed,
has commented on the contrast between Kleist's lengthy paragraphs, which reveal the design of his stories, and Keller's
very short ones, each devoted to a single 'idea', spoken as it
were without pause for breath ('Kleist als Erzähler', *German
Life and Letters*, N.S., VIII, 1, Oct. 1954, p. 29). Keller, it
seems, had little feeling for typographical niceties. In a letter to
Auerbach concerning *Das Fähnlein der sieben Aufrechten*, he
observes that he has simply not noticed punctuation changes
made by Auerbach before publication, 'weil ich überhaupt
mit der Interpunktion auf einem sehr kühlen Fuss stehe'; and a
little later he adds:

> Ich bin auch immer in Verzweiflung wegen der Gänse-
> füsschen im Dialog, den neuen Absätzen etc., etc., weil alles
> das mich nicht intressiert und man doch eine gewisse Ord-
> nung beobachten muss. (15 September 1860)

These typographical differences indicate differing modes of
conducting the narratives, and, ultimately, differing modes of
looking at life and its vicissitudes. In *Das Erdbeben* the paragraphs embody the sudden contrasts of the story: the first is

---

[1] The text of *Kleider machen Leute* in the critical edition by Jonas
Fränkel contains two breaks, one after Strapinski's second meeting with
Nettchen, the other after he falls asleep in the snow. Fränkel omits to
state his authority for these breaks, which do not appear in the first or
other contemporary editions; if they stem from the manuscript, Keller's
attitude to their omission in the printed text is still an open question.
The three sections thus produced would, however, correspond to the
three 'movements' of the story (deception, unmasking, reinstatement).

violent, the second idyllic, the third violent again. In Keller's story the movement from one extreme to the other is a more gradual one; nor are the two extremes themselves, of triumph and disgrace, so far apart. The external structure clearly shows this gentler movement. In Keller, Robert Petsch writes, 'werden die Wendungen und ihre Überbrückungen wohl angedeutet, aber ohne jede Schärfe, mehr auf dem Wege einer allmählichen Umstimmung, einer fast behaglichen Weiterführung auf anderer Ebene und in anderer Atmosphäre' (*Wesen und Formen der Erzählkunst*, 2nd ed., Halle, 1942, p. 152). Such gradual transitions are part of what Oskar Walzel called Keller's 'gedämpfter Ton' (*Gehalt und Gestalt im Kunstwerk des Dichters*, Berlin–Neubabelsberg, 1923, p. 338, cf. p. 213). Moreover, they are peculiarly appropriate, as we shall see, in an account of a man's advance along 'den abschüssigen Weg des Bösen'.

Yet the absence of formal indications of structure certainly does not imply an absence of structure. An important structural system emerges when we look at the time-scale of the story, in the way which recent critics of fiction, notably Günther Müller (*Die Bedeutung der Zeit in der Erzählkunst*, Bonn, 1947), have suggested, and especially when we look at the relationship between the time taken to narrate (*Erzählzeit*) and the time occupied by the action (*Erzählte Zeit*). Whereas the action extends from November ('An einem unfreundlichen Novembertage') to February ('Es war eben Fastnachtszeit'), almost all the narration is concerned with six days only. The story begins with two successive days in November; and it ends with two successive days in February (the day of the sleigh-party and the day of discussions in Seldwyla), followed

by a brief note on subsequent events. These two pairs of days
are narrated at roughly equal length, and together they occupy
some seven-eighths of the book. Between them come the two
days, shortly before Shrovetide, which include the ball, the
engagement of Wenzel and Nettchen, and its approval by her
father. The events of the remainder of the period from November to February are passed over rapidly, or in silence. The
treatment of time in the *Novelle* thus produces a triple structure
with the two outer periods occupying very much more space
than the central one.

This triple structure, however, is modified by the events of
the plot, a detailed examination of which will follow in
Chapter 5. The first pair of days is sub-divided by the decision
to visit Nettchen's father, which introduces a new factor. The
third pair is sub-divided by the revelation of Wenzel's
identity. In this way, the three units of the story become five
—deception, love, engagement, unmasking, reinstatement—
a structure resembling the familiar five acts of drama, with
effective tableaux as the curtain falls at the end of each 'act'.

3. *The Narrator and his Language*

The modes of narration in epic works range from direct
speech and letters—where the narrator acts as a simple record-
ing instrument—through indirect speech, thought sequence,
description and action—where he can flavour his material by
selection or formulation—to overt comment—where he expresses an opinion directly. Keller's narrative manner does not

neglect any of these potentialities; there is none of that concentration on action at the expense of dialogue, description and comment which characterizes Kleist. In *Kleider machen Leute*, two most important sequences—Wenzel's acceptance by Goldach society, and his reconciliation with Nettchen—both contain considerable conversation. Interior monologue records the reactions of Wenzel and Nettchen to the revelation of the tailor's identity. Description is of such importance that it requires a separate chapter. The prevalence of these leisurely modes helps to create 'Das liebenswürdig plaudernde Erzählen Kellers' (von Wiese, 1956, p. 241). Yet with all this there is no shortage of action.

Nor is there any shortage of comment: the attitude of the narrator is the reverse of 'objective', if by this we mean 'in the position of an eye-witness' of the events he narrates. Keller's narrator is rather Olympian, omniscient, aware of his characters' least thoughts, sympathetic and yet superior to them, *in loco parentis*. 'Dies göttliche Umfassen und lächelnde Durchschauen, das den Grundton seiner Werke bildet, scheint mir für Keller wesentlich charakteristisch zu sein', writes Ricarda Huch (1904, p. 51).

Thus the narrator may act as a guide to the milieu of the story, informing us of the historical implications of house-names in Goldach, or commenting on some piece of local colour ('denn da hiess der Tuchhändler noch Tuchherr, der Eisenhändler Eisenherr u.s.w.'). Such comments may take on an ethical tinge, as when he notes the national passion for cards.

This ethical concern also appears whenever the narrator explains the motives of his characters and the consequences of

their actions. Thus he comments on Strapinski's fateful
costume:

> Solcher Habitus war ihm zum Bedürfnis geworden, ohne
> dass er etwas Schlimmes oder Betrügerisches dabei im
> Schilde führte . . .

and on his meek acceptance of the waiter's misunderstanding
of his intention:

> Doch verwickelte er sich jetzt in die erste selbsttätige Lüge,
> weil er in dem verschlossenen Raume ein wenig verweilte,
> und er betrat hiemit den abschüssigen Weg des Bösen.

Observations such as these, which accompany the narrative at
every turn, are a characteristic expression of the paternal attitude in a country where the pedagogic tradition is strong, and
where fiction, from Rousseau through Pestalozzi and Gotthelf
to Keller himself, has long contributed to popular education.
Only rarely (as perhaps in the paragraph on hypocrisy in
princes, prelates, preceptors and painters, which follows
Wenzel's disgrace) do such comments seem irrelevant to the
fiction as a whole.

Keller's narrator, then, is normally omniscient. In *Kleider
machen Leute* he is always so in questions of morality, and
often so in questions of motivation. Yet there are some
important points in the plot at which he is not. The first is
when Wenzel enters the inn:

> Mochte es nun der Mangel an Geistesgegenwart oder an
> Mut sein, den Haufen zu durchbrechen und einfach seines
> Weges zu gehen, — er tat dieses nicht . . .

and there are similar speculations when the coachman identi-
fies him as Graf Strapinski, when Nettchen takes the road

which leads to her lover, and when they finally remove from
Seldwyla to Goldach. The effect of these is clear: they empha-
size the view that in human actions there is sometimes an
element of indeterminacy, of chance; and *Zufall*, we shall see,
is one of the story's themes.

A recent critic writes of these uncertainties: 'Thus Keller
occasionally endangers his own role as the—otherwise—
omniscient author. He poses questions or suggests possible
interpretations in instances where he alone can really be
informed' (Audrey Flandreau, 'A Study of Ricarda Huch's
Novellen with special reference to Keller', *Germanic Review*,
XXV, 1950, p. 36). But author and narrator are ontologically
distinct: that is, they exist in quite different senses. The author
is a historical person, the narrator a fictional character like any
other. By confusing the two, Flandreau prevents herself from
considering the function of the narrator's ignorance at these
important points.—This distinction of status between author
and narrator does not, of course, mean that their views are
always or even normally at variance one with the other. In
Keller's case, the narrator's attitude generally differs from the
author's own only in the way that the simplicity and clarity of
art differs from the complexity and confusion of life.

So much for the narrator's explicit comments. A narrator,
however, may convey an opinion by the tone of his language
as well as by what he says. His choices of syntax, vocabulary
and figures of speech are all significant. The language of a
story is the narrator's (or the characters', in direct speech) as
well as the writer's, just as the language of a play is the characters' as well as the dramatist's.

On the whole, Keller is not particularly concerned to

characterize the language of his characters. One exception to this is the use of expletives, seen here in the exchanges between innkeeper and cook during the preparation and serving of Strapinski's meal. The contrast between the honest innkeeper ('Ins drei Teufels Namen!', 'Zum Teufel', 'Hol mich der Teufel') and the would-be deceitful cook ('Ei der Tausend', 'Gelobt sei Jesus Christ', 'darauf wollt ich schwören, wenn es nicht verboten wäre!') is particularly pleasant. Appropriately enough, too, the ponderous phrasing of official language (*Kanzleistil*), familiar to Keller in his capacity as Cantonal Clerk, is used in reporting the opinion of Nettchen's father, the local magistrate, that Strapinski's marriage must not delay him 'in seinen Geschäften und vorhabenden Reisen'. Perhaps something of the official manner has rubbed off onto Nettchen, to judge from the formality with which she enumerates her grounds for going ahead with her marriage. Occasionally, too, a character will employ a word with a dialect flavour, as when Böhni speaks of a 'Goldacher Putsch'—a word of Swiss origin.

Keller was, of course, a Swiss, and his native language was the German of Zürich. He wrote, however, in Standard German, and the effort of doing so may account for the extensive revision he found necessary, and for an occasional cumbersomeness of phrasing, especially in dialogue. In general the style is a written one, with participles, especially the present participle, much in evidence:

> Nach diesem Hofe fuhr Nettchen jetzt, von der Strasse ablenkend und mit einem kräftigen Peitschenknallen vor dem Hause haltend.

Dialect as such does not appear, but occasionally words or

phrases are used in a slang connotation (e.g. 'fechten' = 'to beg', in the idiom of the journeymen) or with a local flavour, Alemannic ('von dannen', 'Sauser') or specifically Swiss ('sein Ränzchen voll zu packen', 'auf den Stockzähnen lächelnd'). These features are not expressive of attitude, but through them the narrator acquires a Swiss quality suited to the story's setting.

An easy-going attitude is, however, expressed by the absence of exaggeration. The vocabulary is free of extremes. The syntax flows easily; rhetorical devices, repetition and antithesis, are largely avoided, and little use is made of the capacity of the German language for involution and subordination, which in the hands of a writer like Kleist becomes a tool for the exploration and surveying of experience.

The narrator, too, is down-to-earth, practical, matter-of-fact. When Nettchen expresses her determination to remain faithful to Strapinski he observes:

> Doch war sie keineswegs so blöde, dieses Schicksal nicht selbst ein wenig lenken zu wollen; vielmehr fasste sie rasch und keck neue Entschlüsse.

It is characteristic of him to bring fine feeling and blunt language together in this way. The phrasing, too, has a colloquial flavour, with its asides and revised formulations ('Das Fechten fiel ihm äusserst schwer, ja schien ihm gänzlich unmöglich'). Among the figures of speech, down-to-earth realism and plasticity may manifest itself simply in the choice of a verb, or result in an extended image in the Homeric manner:

> ... dazu trank er den Wein in tüchtigen Zügen und steckte grosse Brotbissen in den Mund; kurz, es war eine so

B

hastig belebte Einfuhr, wie wenn bei aufsteigendem
Gewitter das Heu von der nahen Wiese gleich auf der
Gabel in die Scheune geflüchtet wird.

Such similes are often humorous in effect:

Also ging der Mantelträger ohne Widerspruch, sanft wie
ein Lämmlein . . .

. . . das Schneiderblütchen fing in der Nähe des Frauen-
zimmers an, seine Sprünge zu machen und seinen Reiter
davonzutragen.

Other metaphors used by the narrator relate specifically to
the story's themes. Thus one series, the images of artistic
illusion, point the unreality of Wenzel's initial success:

Denn eine neue Wendung war eingetreten, ein Fräulein
beschritt den Schauplatz der Ereignisse.

. . . während er bisher nichts getan hatte, um im geringsten
in die Rolle einzugehen, die man ihm aufbürdete . . .

Dies Bild arbeitete er weiter aus . . .

—a series which ends with Nettchen's cry: 'Keine Romane
mehr!'

Other images invoke directly the story's theme of essence
and appearance. A connection is made between Wenzel's
costume and his hunger:

. . . also dass er der Märtyrer seines Mantels war und
Hunger litt, so schwarz wie des letztern Sammetfutter.

Surface and contents are linked in the image used when
Wenzel emerges from the coach:

. . . Kinder und Nachbaren . . . neugierig, welch ein Kern
sich aus so unerhörter Schale enthülsen werde . . .

whilst that accompanying Wenzel's second meeting with Nettchen underlines the parallel between environment and personality once again:

> Mit jedem Tage wandelte er sich, gleich einem Regenbogen, der zusehends bunter wird an der vorbrechenden Sonne. Er lernte in Stunden, in Augenblicken, was Andere nicht in Jahren, da es in ihm gesteckt hatte, wie das Farbenwesen im Regentropfen.

The paternal attitude of the narrator to his characters is also reflected in his language, especially, as Ricarda Huch observed long ago, in his fondness for diminutives—in origin, again, the survival of a regional feature. Their use emphasizes the difference in maturity between narrator and characters, whether it be 'Nettchen', or Wenzel—'ein armes Schneiderlein' with his 'Schnurrbärtchen', his 'Ränzchen', and his 'handgrosses Bündelein' with its 'Büchschen Pomade'—or Böhni with his 'Backenbärtchen' and his silver 'Döschen'.

At the same time as thus reducing his characters in stature, the narrator also tends to elevate them, by what Stuart Atkins has called his 'mock-heroic treatment' (1944, p. 100). This includes the use of words of foreign origin ('Falliment', 'Habitus', 'desperat') and somewhat precious circumlocutions ('Sausergelüste büssen', 'sich ergehen', 'ein historisch-ethnographischer Schneiderfestzug', 'Nahtbeflissenen'). The resulting hyperbole can hardly be other than ironic. The use of sobriquets ('der Mantelträger' for Strapinski) and of epithets ('die ruhige Köchin', 'der wackere Wirt') also recalls an epic manner in mock-heroic guise.

A similar tendency is apparent in the images comparing

Wenzel to princes and heroes (and in one case to the eagle, a regal bird):

> So sass er denn wie ein kränkelnder Fürst, vor welchem die Hofleute ein angenehmes Schauspiel aufführen und den Lauf der Welt darstellen.

> Da stand er nun, gleich dem Jüngling am Scheidewege [Hercules], auf einer wirklichen Kreuzstrasse . . .

> . . . sein Mantel umschlug die schlanke, stolze, schneeweisse Gestalt des Mädchens wie mit schwarzen Adlersflügeln . . .

> Das Paar aber sass unbeweglich auf seinen Stühlen gleich einem steinernen ägyptischen Königspaar, ganz still und einsam; man glaubte den unabsehbaren glühenden Wüstensand zu fühlen.

It is well known that Keller employs incongruous images of this kind— *Märchenvergleiche*, as Fleissner calls them—in other works. Their incongruity is a source of humour; the mock heroic tone reminds us of the heights to which Strapinski aspires, and the gulf which separates him from them.

And yet: the nature of irony is ambivalence, fondness and criticism mixed. For a staunch old republican like Keller especially, who was as likely to be mock-heroic about kings as about tailors, and in a *Novelle* where the mock hero turns into a real hero, these images also convey, within the irony, an intimation of the noble nature of the two lovers, as they do of those other lovers in *Romeo und Julia auf dem Dorfe*. They thus express more obliquely the comment of Grillparzer's narrator in *Der arme Spielmann*:

> Von dem Wortwechsel weinerhitzter Karrenschieber spinnt sich ein unsichtbarer, aber ununterbrochener Faden bis zum

Zwist der Göttersöhne, und in der jungen Magd, die, halb
wider Willen, dem drängenden Liebhaber seitab vom
Gewühl der Tanzenden folgt, liegen als Embryo die Julien,
die Didos und die Medeen,

or the theoretical statement by Stifter in the famous preface to
Bunte Steine.

4. *Description and Symbol*

The precision of Keller's presentation of physical reality,
especially in the visual sphere, has long been recognized, and
critics have pointed to the influence of his early training as a
painter. Yet the characteristic is one he shares with contemporary writers—Mörike, Stifter, Droste-Hülshoff, Gotthelf,
Otto Ludwig, Storm, Raabe—who have become known as
Poetic Realists.

The detailed and lengthy account of some aspect of physical
reality which, at first glance, may not appear to be central to
his theme, is so frequent that Keller has often been accused of
inartistic digressions. A famous example is the enumeration of
Züs Bünzlin's possessions, in the earlier Seldwyla story *Die
drei gerechten Kammmacher*. In *Kleider machen Leute* the description of the houses of Goldach, with their curious names, is
matched by the account of the meal he is given at the inn, with
successive courses and accompanying wines set out in detail:
even the types of tobacco offered afterwards by the admiring
citizens are differentiated precisely. Shorter but no less precise
are the descriptions of the procession of sleighs and of the
mime presented by the inhabitants of Seldwyla.

Keller has a special fondness for the sequence of items set down without comment. One such list occurs during the account of Wenzel's dispatch of the partridge pasty: 'Fleisch, Trüffeln, Klösschen, Boden, Deckel, alles schlang er ohne Ansehen der Person hinunter . . .' A particularly good example of his eye for detail—one editor, Nussberger, calls it 'genre painting'—is the list of contents of Strapinski's lost bundle, 'das ein Schnupftuch, eine Haarbürste, einen Kamm, ein Büchschen Pomade und einen Stengel Bartwichse enthielt'.

The aspects of physical reality which Keller describes include not only houses, vehicles, personal belongings and food, examples of which we have seen already, but also the weather, clothing, personal appearance, names, and attitude or gesture. He also enjoys depicting processions and festivities, especially those with an element of masquerade. Nature, on the other hand—the animals and plants portrayed with love and knowledge by Stifter, Droste-Hülshoff or Storm—is relatively unimportant to Keller, who tends to describe only the broader aspects of natural landscape, and to reserve his detail for objects more intimately associated with man. The reader of *Kleider machen Leute*, at least, will find it difficult to see how Otto Luterbacher could claim that 'Kellers Fabeln spielen sich fast ausschliesslich im Freien ab; selten finden sich Szenen im Innern eines Hauses' (*Die Landschaft in Gottfried Kellers Prosawerken*, Tübingen, 1911, p. 13), and will agree rather with Robert Saitschik that 'Die Landschaftsbilder sind hier gleichwie in allen anderen Novellen Kellers kurz gehalten, desto eingehender die Genrebilder' (*Meister der Schweizerischen Dichtung des neunzehnten Jahrhunderts*, Frauenfeld, 1894, p. 166).

An obvious function of this detailed description is to create the illusion of life, so that the reader, recognizing as familiar the world to which he is introduced, will achieve more readily that 'suspension of disbelief' which is called for in art. In fact, as Auerbach pointed out in his review of the first volume of *Die Leute von Seldwyla* (*Allgemeine Zeitung, Beilage*, 17 April 1856), apropos of the narrator's insistence on the 'truth' of his story in the opening paragraph of *Romeo und Julia auf dem Dorfe*, Keller himself was not entirely clear about the relationship of actual reality to fictional reality: he simply assumed that if what he presented was drawn from life, it would be fictionally convincing. An interesting example of his insistence on the actuality of his own descriptions occurs in a letter to Storm of 25 June 1878, discussing the sleigh-procession in *Kleider machen Leute*:

> Schon früher hat mir ein norddeutscher Kritiker einen grotesken Fastnachtszug (Schneider-Schlittenfahrt) als ganz unmöglich, ungeheuerlich und daher unzulässig bezeichnet, während hierzulande dergleichen nicht einmal auffällt, weil es jeder erlebt hat.

Moreover, Keller finds little need to refine reality before presenting it in his stories. He allows Wenzel to be directed to 'eine gewisse Bequemlichkeit' (some of his editors have been more prudish), and Nettchen to blow her nose 'heartily' before setting off after her lover. It is amusing to discover that this was arraigned by a contemporary critic, on the grounds that, although ladies are known to blow their noses, they need not do so in books (Jakob Mähly, 'Gottfried Keller', *Die Gegenwart*, XXXVIII, 1890, p. 134).

Descriptive passages often embody a turning-point in the

plot, too, as Paul Wüst, author of the first detailed study of *Kleider machen Leute*, points out. This is certainly true of the masquerade, which is directly concerned with the unmasking of 'Graf' Strapinski, and of that other set-piece, the great meal at the opening of the story, where Wenzel's specific reactions to the various courses and wines set before him are an important factor in confirming his identity as a nobleman.

Description is also a considerable source of humour. The contrast between Strapinski's meagre possessions when the story opens, and the extravagant presents he receives on the following morning, is intensified by the detail in which they are depicted; and the bizarre nature of many items is a source of humour in itself—a kind of local humour, independent of the story as a whole. There are some good instances of this in the list of house-names.

In addition to these three functions, description also has a symbolic aspect. This comes out clearly in the colour adjectives. At times, they convey visual precision: the soup is 'die braungoldene Brühe', and the new wine is 'karneolfarbig'. Joachim Ziesenitz has shown, however, that the greater part of the colour is symbolic rather than simply pictorial. At the opening, Strapinski is characterized by black ('über seinem schwarzen Sonntagskleide', 'einen weiten dunkelgrauen Radmantel', 'mit schwarzem Sammt ausgeschlagen', 'lange schwarze Haare', 'mit . . . seinen dunklen Augen'), relieved only by his pallor. Indeed, at times he recalls that mysterious and daemonic emissary of the dark powers, the 'Schwarzer Geiger' in *Romeo und Julia auf dem Dorfe*. Black contrasts with the whiteness of the snow, and with the whiteness associated with Nettchen, until, at the moment of the declaration of their love, it almost drives out white:

> Er bedeckte ihre glühenden Wangen mit seinen fein duf-
> tenden dunklen Locken und sein Mantel umschlug die
> schlanke, stolze, schneeweisse Gestalt des Mädchens wie mit
> schwarzen Adlersflügeln . . .

almost a vampire image, despite the narrator's assertion that:

> es war ein wahrhaft schönes Bild, das seine Berechtigung
> ganz allein in sich selbst zu tragen schien.

Not until white triumphs once more when Wenzel lies down in the snow to die, and is rescued by Nettchen ('ganz in weisses Pelzwerk gehüllt'), can the promise of his costume for the sleigh-party ('in einem polnischen Überrock von grünem Sammet'—changed by Keller from 'schwarzem' in the manuscript) be achieved. Nettchen's 'blaue Schleier' are also significant: they suggest at once the object of Romantic yearning and the possibility of forgiveness [cf. the veil as a symbol of mercy at the end of Brentano's *Geschichte vom braven Kasperl und dem schönen Annerl* (1817)].

Symbolism may also take the form of a parallel between environment and fate, illustrated in the four phases of Wenzel's fortunes. At the beginning, the weather is inclement, with snow and rain; he is on foot; he is on the road; he is hungry; his belongings are few; and his physical attitude is dejected. When he is accepted, the sun comes out, he rides in carriages and sleighs and on horseback, lives in comfortable houses, eats excellent meals, is showered with gifts, and walks with confidence. After his disgrace, he goes out once more into the hostile snow, on foot, in the forest, as penniless and unencumbered as when he came, and just as dejected. And when, finally, Nettchen rescues him, the emphasis moves from snow to moonlight, he rides once more by sleigh, moves back to the indoor world, acquires possessions and positions by his marriage, and holds up his head. Mathilde Eppmann (1953) reviews in detail the reflections of Wenzel's fortunes in his bodily attitude, and this has since been summed up by Ziesenitz as follows:

> (Wandern, schreiten, galoppieren—davonstehlen, wandeln, taumeln — ohne Umsehen gehen, stolz schreiten.) So gelangen wir zu einer überschaubaren Linie. Aufstieg, Fall und Neubeginn zeichnen sich deutlich auf ihr ab. (1955, p. 415)

Nettchen's gestures are equally revealing. When she rescues Strapinski from the snow, it is she who drives the sleigh; when they leave the farm after reaching their new understanding, she restores the reins to him.

Such parallels are found in all the stories in *Die Leute von Seldwyla*. But in *Kleider machen Leute* they are of special interest: as the title suggests, the *Novelle* deals directly with the relationship between personal character and physical appearance. The 'Radmantel', indeed, becomes a leitmotif of the story. The fact that Strapinski is taken for a nobleman in the first place is due to the impression made on the inn-keeper and his staff, and later the citizens of Goldach, by his possession of a carriage, his outward appearance, and his hesitant and 'refined' conduct. Later events seem at first to invalidate this parallel; but by the end of the story a meaningful relationship between external and internal features is re-established.

This relationship is taken up again when Strapinski, while walking round Goldach, reflects on the connection between the names of the houses and the nature of their occupants. This is, of course, in part a joke at Strapinski's expense. Yet in the end the last laugh is his, for his further speculation on the name of the inn at which he is staying—'zur Waage genannt' —is justified, in part at least, by later events:

> So war er geneigt zu glauben, die wunderliche Aufnahme, welche er gefunden, hänge hiermit im Zusammenhang, so dass z.B. das Sinnbild der Waage, in welcher er wohnte, bedeute, dass dort das ungleiche Schicksal abgewogen und ausgeglichen und zuweilen ein reisender Schneider zum Grafen gemacht würde.

The inns to which Nettchen and Wenzel go on their arrival in Seldwyla—'zum Regenbogen' and 'den Wilden Mann' respectively—are equally symbolic. The rainbow appears earlier as a metaphor indicative of fortune; now, by its association with Nettchen, this significance is strengthened through its link to the similarly significant name of the sleigh in which hero and heroine travel, 'die Fortuna'. It is also interesting to note that, according to his editor Jonas Fränkel, Keller considered at least two alternatives to 'Teich Bethesda' (John v. 2 ff.) as the name of Böhni's sleigh: 'Thal Josaphat' (Joel iii. 2, 12, 14) and 'Brunnen Rogel' (2 Sam. xvii. 17).

In the early part of the story, two incidents relate Wenzel's fate even more specifically to the physical world about him. The first is pointed out by Ziesenitz: when the coachman, at the top of the hill, offers Strapinski a lift, the latter accepts, 'worauf der Wagen rasch mit ihm von dannen rollte . . .' From this point his fate begins to run away with him; and it runs downhill. This is not the only parallel between coach and 'count': the hollowness of the latter is symbolized by the fact that the coach 'schien .. schwer bepackt zu sein, obgleich alles leer war'.

The second incident occurs during the preparation of the meal. The innkeeper is worried because his partridge pie is reserved for diners expected later, and is not large enough for Strapinski to share. The cook proposes that Wenzel should be given first cut at it, and that what is left should be supplemented by the judicious admixture of minced chops.

Doch der wackere Wirt sagte ernsthaft: 'Köchin, ich habe Euch schon einmal gesagt, dass dergleichen in dieser Stadt und in diesem Hause nicht angeht! Wir leben hier solid und ehrenfest und vermögen es!'

'Ei der Tausend, ja, ja!' rief die Köchin endlich etwas aufgeregt, 'wenn man sich denn nicht zu helfen weiss, so opfere man die Sache! Hier sind zwei Schnepfen, die ich den Augenblick vom Jäger gekauft habe, die kann man am Ende der Pastete zusetzen. Eine mit Schnepfen gefälschte Rebhuhnpastete werden die Leckermäuler nicht beanstanden!'

Keller perhaps had in mind here the idiomatic sense of 'Pastete' ('eine verwickelte, unangenehme Geschichte', Grimm); at any rate, is is difficult not to draw a parallel between spurious and genuine in partridge pasties and in Polish counts, and to conclude that Strapinski himself is 'eine mit Schnepfen gefälschte Rebhuhnpastete'—a substitute equal to or better than the original—which Nettchen, like any other *Leckermaul*, will not ultimately refuse.

In symbols such as these, plasticity and significance are fused, through the process which Keller himself, using an image borrowed from F. T. Vischer, describes as 'das Didaktische im Poetischen aufzulösen, wie Zucker oder Salz im Wasser . . .' (to Auerbach, 25 February 1860).

5. Plot, Character and Themes

Much critical ingenuity has been devoted to defining the *Novelle*. Now, however, there are signs of a more sceptical approach: a recent seminar under Emil Staiger cautiously concluded that the *Novelle* is 'eine Erzählung mittlerer Länge'! It might be more useful to reach a definition by reference to other genres. Within the wider genre *prose epic*, the *Novelle* belongs to the category *short story* (*Erzählung*), distinguished from the more substantial *novel* in that it deals with a single situation (and its antecedents and consequences) and from the less substantial *anecdote* in that it goes beyond the bare bones of events. Within the *short story*, the Novelle belongs to the *realistic short story*, distinguished from the *Märchen* in that the supernatural does not dominate its motivation. Within the *realistic short story*, the *Novelle* is distinguished by the novelty or striking quality of the situation it presents. We thus arrive at what Goethe succinctly formulated as 'eine sich ereignete, unerhörte Begebenheit' (to Eckermann, 29 January 1827).

Such distinctions do not produce entirely discrete categories, any more than do other similar genre distinctions (even that between prose and verse). Nevertheless, they are not without value, provided we use them to help us understand, not reject, the fiction we encounter. The distinction between *Märchen* and realistic short story, for example, will be needed in our final chapter. The question of novelty is also relevant. Benno von Wiese asserts that the story 'berichtet zwar keine alltägliche, gewiss aber auch keine unerhörte Begebenheit' (1956, p. 239). But we must not take 'unerhört' too literally, or only plots as violent as Kleist's will qualify. It is surely the merit of Stifter, in the preface to *Bunte Steine*, to have shown that novelty is relative; it does not take an earthquake to startle a village. For the inhabitants of Goldach, these events are indubitably 'unerhört'; this is shown by the news-value of the real-life events which in part provided Keller's source.

The basic theme of the story is that of the relation between essence and appearance, being and seeming, *Sein* and *Schein*. Hardly novel in itself; but when it is exemplified by the transformation of an out-of-work tailor into a Polish count, it begins to seem more intriguing. Chance puts Strapinski into this position, and chance, usually in the enchanting shape of Nettchen, repeatedly prevents his attempts at escape. Keller gives the old theme further twists. Strapinski's assumption of his new rôle is passive rather than active: to escape would require a strength of purpose he does not possess. He slides, rather than strides, down 'den abschüssigen Weg des Bösen'. In this respect, the story forms a sharp contrast to *Der Schmied seines Glückes*, whose hero John Kabys deliberately assumes the manner of a gentleman. Moreover, Strapinski is actively encouraged to develop his deception by the snobbery and secret longings of the burghers of Goldach, including Nettchen. On the one hand, therefore, he is an innocent deceiver.

On the other hand, the rôle which fate thrusts upon him is one which corresponds to something in his own nature—an

impetus to refinement, the desire, as he later puts it to Nettchen, 'etwas Ordentliches zu sein oder zu scheinen'. This
Romantic yearning is the result of inheritance from his mother
and environmental influence during his childhood. It leads him
to cultivate his appearance in a manner alien to his position in
society—'und zwar unabhängig von Zweck und Nutzen, nur
aus einer ästhetischen Grundhaltung' (von Wiese, 1956,
p. 244)—and, in the last analysis, prevents him from revealing
his 'real' status. But it also means that in a sense he is not an
impostor at all.

Paula Ritzler has argued that, whereas in writers like Kleist
calamities result from external events, in Keller they are due to
the hero's character. The precarious situation reached by the
mid-point of *Kleider machen Leute*, however, is due both to the
opportunities provided by chance—represented in part by his
fellow human-beings, irascible coachman, honest innkeeper,
sly fellow-suitor and impressionable Nettchen—and to
Strapinski's reaction to them. This interplay of character and
situation is typical of Keller.

Yet although Wenzel is thus not exclusively to blame for
the situation in which he finds himself, it is he alone who is
held to account for it. Three stanzas from Keller's satirical
poem *Der Apotheker von Chamounix* (1860) offer an illuminat-
ing commentary on this expiation:

> Denn die Schlimmen, die mit frommen
> Worten einst die Welt betrogen,
> Mit Gebarung der Gerechten,
> Braten ewig in der Hölle.
>
> Doch die Guten, die in schlimme
> Sitten einst sich eingewickelt,

Müssen sich von diesen rein'gen,
Bis sie weiss sind wie der Montblanc.

Nicht der Wolf im Lämmleinspelze
Ist allein ein schlechter Tartüffe;
Auch das Lamm im Tigerfelle
Macht sich arger Sünde schuldig.

(I. vii. 17–28)

The sudden turn, at the moment of his disgrace, forces the
hero, and the reader, to an awareness of the tragic implications
of a situation whose comic side has hitherto been paramount.

The escape from this apparent impasse provides the last and
most intriguing novelty of the story. The possibility of escape
is furnished by Nettchen, who also has her share of Romantic
impulses, witness her determination to marry 'nur einen
Italiener oder einen Polen, einen grossen Pianisten oder einen
Räuberhauptmann mit schönen Locken'. Her 'Keine Romane
mehr!' finally overcomes the impulses of phantasy, and the
way is open for Strapinski's reinstatement. Boeschenstein
observes that the discussion leading to this resolution signifi-
cantly takes place in the simple farm-house. This is one hint
that the conclusion of the story does not represent a submission
to the forces of convention; we cannot say simply: 'Aus dem
romantischen, träumerischen Sonderling ist ein tüchtiger
Bürger geworden' (Herman Meyer, *Der Typus des Sonderlings
in der deutschen Literatur*, Amsterdam, 1943, p. 149). A solution
is made possible, not only by the promise of honest endeavour,
but also by the presence of humanity and love: Nettchen, the
dominant partner as the woman so often is in Keller, recog-
nizes that Wenzel, if less than a count, is more than a tailor;
though not a nobleman, he is a noble man.

The contrast with the end of *Romeo und Julia auf dem Dorfe* is instructive. Vrenchen, like Nettchen, rejects the Romantic outlet, provided in her case by life with the gypsies. But for her there is no positive solution: it is blocked by the workings both of fate—the lack of a secure social standing—and of character—Sali's violence, resulting in the injury to Marti. Yet *Romeo und Julia* is an exception in Keller's works: whenever possible he reintegrates his characters into society. Strapinski's faults, though serious, are human after all, springing from embarrassment and love, and not from calculation. 'Und wo Keller irgend ein Unwesen mit einem noch so dünnen goldenen Bändchen noch an die Menschlichkeit gebunden findet, da rettet er es in diese hinüber kraft seiner dichterischen Machtvollkommenheit . . .' (Wüst, 1914, p. 109).

Johannes Klein, in his history of the German *Novelle*, sums up the story as follows: 'Das ist die Stilfigur des Chiasmus, des X. Nur der erste Teil der Novelle hat das Thema des Titels, der zweite das Gegenthema.' Other critics say that the first half of the work is comic, the second serious. But this is over-simplified; the proverb of the title is first inverted, but then doubly proved: once in the sense that Wenzel's Polish personality makes his emotional fortune and leads to his marriage; and once again in the sense that the tailoring business makes his financial fortune. The structure of the plot is thus not simply antithetical, but antithesis followed by synthesis.

The rôle of the disappointed lover, Melchior Böhni, deserves a note. 'Boehni ist eine Art Mephistonatur, die das Böse tut und das Gute schafft' (Ziesenitz, 1955, p. 422); and in this he takes over the function exercised originally by the

C

coachman. He recalls the bloodless justness of *Die drei gerechten Kammmacher;* but in him it is relieved by the element of humour.

'Wenn [Keller] erzählt, denkt er stets an das Ganze und darum finden sich bei ihm auch im einzelnen immer die Spuren des Gedankens, welcher das Ganze erfüllt' (Hellmuth Mielke, revd. Hans Joachim Homann, *Der deutsche Roman des 19. und 20. Jahrhunderts,* 7th ed., Dresden, 1920, p. 137). We have seen examples of this reflection in our study of vocabulary, imagery and symbolic description. More striking still is the proliferation of abstract leitmotifs—those repeated words, adjective or noun, which carry the themes of the story. One complex of these relates to essence and appearance in the sphere of nobility and decency. At first it is Strapinski's appearance which attracts the epithets *edel, sorgfältig, still, bescheiden, ehrwürdig, ordentlich, vornehm, höflich, prächtig, nüchtern, ehrfurchtsvoll,* etc; but soon they extend to his behaviour and his character, and we realize, before his disgrace and long before his reinstatement, that the hero is a gentleman. Decency and honesty appear in other contexts too. We have noted already the innkeeper's refusal to allow sharp practice; the problem of trust reappears in his promise to his late wife not to allow the keys of the inn out of his hands. Altogether, as Ziesenitz observes, he is very close to Strapinski. Through these leitmotifs, too, Wenzel's personality is linked to the solid civic order which eventually absorbs him and which is characterized by such epithets as *stattlich, vornehm, prächtig, reich.*

The other main theme of the story is that of chance, and this also appears as a leitmotif with *Zufall, Schicksal, Glück* and *Unglück.* The first mention of *Glück* associates it with 'der goldenen Freiheit der Landstrasse'; but soon it is something Wenzel can only achieve by maintaining his deception. At the moment of his disgrace, *Glück* is driven out by *Unglück*, and it is only when Nettchen accepts him back that the lost fortune of his childhood, the false fortune of the 'Graf' and the misfortune of his disgrace give way to true fortune, prefigured in the name of house and sleigh, 'Fortuna'. The narrator's emphasis on chance in the motivation of the story has been discussed already. Its importance is underlined by the repetition, noted by Ziesenitz, of the word *rasch* (with its suggestion of unpremeditated action). The plot itself rests upon a series of coincidences—Strapinski's Polish name and cavalry service, his luck at cards and in the lottery, his knowledge of a Polish song, Nettchen's newly achieved majority, and especially the chance resemblance between Nettchen and Strapinski's childhood friend.[1] There is no need to see in these coincidences, as Wüst does, evidence that *Kleider machen Leute* was originally conceived as a dramatic comedy. Nor it is possible to agree with Stuart Atkins that 'Keller perhaps intended a travesty of conventional belletristic romanticism' (1944, p. 97). Had he done so, he could not have allowed chance so great a part in the final rehabilitation of Strapinski. It is rather that, in society as he conceives it—though not as Goldach or Seldwyla normally embody it—there is a place for the workings of those unpredictable factors which we call chance. An irrational element is carried over into the otherwise rigorously ordered bourgeois world.

[1] There is no evidence for the assumption by Stuart Atkins that Nettchen *is* the childhood friend, and a great deal of evidence against it.

6. Fact and Fable

In his review of the first Seldwyla stories, Auerbach observed:

> Es ist ein Product der *realistischen Dichtung*, und schon indem man diese beiden Worte in Einen Begriff fasst, sollte alsbald erkannt seyn dass hier weder Realistik — die blosse gemeine Wirklichkeit allein — noch auch die Dichtung allein, als reine Phantastik gedacht, dem Werke seinen Ursprung gab.

The duality expressed here, or in Otto Ludwig's term *poetischer Realismus*, has continued to preoccupy critics. While the majority have arrived at a view of Keller which includes both aspects, there have also been attempts to claim him exclusively for one or other extreme. The critic Emil Brenning, for example, writes: 'Keller ist einer der grössten Realisten unter den Schriftstellern' (*Gottfried Keller*, Bremen, 1892, p. 58); the novelist Theodor Fontane asserts the opposite:

> Gottfried Keller, und dies erklärt alles, ist au fond ein Märchenerzähler . . . Er erzählt nicht aus einem bestimmten Jahrhundert, kaum aus einem bestimmten Lande, gewiss nicht aus ständisch gegliederten und deshalb sprachlich verschiedenen Verhältnissen heraus, sondern hat für seine Darstellung eine im *wesentlichen sich gleichbleibende Märchensprache* . . .
>
> ('Die Leute von Seldwyla', *Gesammelte Werke*, 2nd S., IX, Berlin, [1910], pp. 250–1)

Keller himself stresses now one and now the other of these sides. With the sleigh-procession, we have seen, he is insistent

on actuality, the observed quality. But in a letter to Paul
Heyse, three years later, he writes:

> Im stillen nenne ich dergleichen die Reichsunmittelbarkeit
> der Poesie, d.h. das Recht, zu jeder Zeit, auch im Zeitalter
> des Fracks und der Eisenbahnen, an das Parabelhafte, das
> Fabelmässige ohne weiteres anzuknüpfen, ein Recht, das
> man sich nach meiner Meinung durch keine Kulturwand-
> lungen nehmen lassen soll. (27 July 1881)

Both considerations are present in the narrator's introduction
to *Romeo und Julia auf dem Dorfe:*

> Diese Geschichte zu erzählen würde eine müssige Nachah-
> mung sein, wenn sie nicht auf einem wirklichen Vorfall
> beruhte, zum Beweise, wie tief im Menschenleben jede
> jener Fabeln wurzelt, auf welche die grossen alten Werke
> gebaut sind. Die Zahl solcher Fabeln ist mässig; aber stets
> treten sie in neuem Gewande wieder in die Erscheinung und
> zwingen alsdann die Hand, sie festzuhalten.

This emphasis on a combination of actual and archetype,
characterizing Keller even more than his fellow Poetic Realists,
helps to account for his great indebtedness to sources, actual
and literary—a surprising fact about this highly individual
writer. In the case of *Kleider machen Leute*, for example, the
reader might well suppose that the material was invented by
Keller on a hint provided by the proverb of the title. Nothing
could be further from the truth.

Important source-material from life was provided by incidents which had occurred in contemporary Switzerland. At
Winterthur, in the late 1830's, the Polish Count Sobansky, a
political refugee, was imposed on by a young man claiming to
be the son of an acquaintance, Count Normann of Baden, in
hiding because of a duel he had fought. The young man

moved in local society, but then robbed his acquaintances and disappeared in a borrowed sleigh. He proved to be a young gamekeeper, dismissed by Normann. This incident supplied the motifs 'Polish count', 'manners learned in subordinate capacity' and 'social success', with some other details.

The 'tailor' motif derives from another incident which took place about 1844 and is recounted by Arnold Ruge ('Die Komödie in Wädenschwyl am Zürichsee', *Gesammelte Schriften*, Mannheim, X, 1848, pp. 156–79). A young man and his 'mother' (actually a tailor and an actress) appeared as Graf and Gräfin Stechenheim; they were accepted; the 'count' had love-affairs and disappeared after a final feast, leaving returned love-letters and unpaid debts. The story was acted by the neighbouring town of Richterswyl the following Shrove Tuesday. This incident also suggested the motifs 'engagement', 'revelation at a feast', and 'Shrove Tuesday mime'.

Keller was able to fill out the Polish aspect from more personal material. He had been sympathetic to Polish refugees since his boyhood, when one had lodged with the family. During the Polish Revolution of 1863/64, he became Secretary to the *Schweizerisches Central-Comité für Polen*, and as such had had to compose a letter warning other refugee committees against a certain Julius Schramm, a Prussian who had been secretary to the President of the Central Committee. Schramm claimed to have fled because of a duel; when it turned out that there was little truth in his story, he was discredited. Another Polish 'refugee' at this time, Julian Saminski, was arrested as a Russian spy; a third, Count Stroynowski, engaged in dubious activities. Margarete Rothbarth argues persuasively that these figures gave Keller models for Strapinski: we know that in the original manuscript the latter's name often appears as Julian, and his origin is more specifically East Prussian than in the published version.

Other details in the story are based on personal observation. Many of the names occur in Zürich (among them the inn-names 'Zur Waage' and 'Der Wilde Mann'). The actuality of the sleigh-procession has already been noted. Other customs too, are typically Swiss: Boeschenstein points to the almost forcible entertainment of the stranger, and to the drinking-party following immediately after coffee. There is a parallel to the *Sauser*-tasting, in a letter to Heyse of 3 November 1859: 'wir halten die Sitzungen in einem Wirtshause, wo wir einen trüblich karneolfarbigen Weinmost trinken, alle Tage frisch vom Lande hereinkommend'. Moreover, Wenzel's 'Radmantel' was part of Keller's own wardrobe during the Munich period, and his initial journey recalls Keller's rather crestfallen return from Munich to Zürich, also in November; many critics, indeed, have made comparisons between hero and author, especially in their Romantic inclinations. Keller's fondness for what the psycho-analyst Eduard Hitschmann called the 'half-family' (Wenzel and mother, Nettchen and father) is also autobiographical: Keller lost his father at the age of five.

Literary analogues have been examined by critics from Bächtold to Hennig, most fully by Wüst. The theme of the tailor who makes his fortune has a long history. The tailor works indoors, is often pale and delicate, and dresses well, so that of all manual workers he is best adapted to enter polite society: his urge to rise is thus a favoured theme. It appears among the *Märchen* of the brothers Grimm, and in Romantic works—in Brentano's *Märchen vom Schneider Siebentot auf einen Schlag*, and in poems by Heine ('Traumbilder VIII', in *Buch der Lieder*) and Chamisso ('Kleidermacher-Mut').

Other Romantic versions provide much closer parallels with *Kleider machen Leute*. Tieck's *Leben des berühmten Kaisers Abraham Tonelli* (1798) deals with the son of poor parents, apprenticed to a tailor, with a taste for delicate food, who is employed by a Polish nobleman, taken for a duke by an inn-keeper, and eventually makes his fortune. In *Die schwarze Spinne* (1819), by August Langbein, the devil's tailor appears as a Crown Prince, woos the daughter of a local burgher, and is unmasked at a feast; his costume resembles Strapinski's, and the Devil observes at one point: 'Dass doch in Eurer elenden Welt immer das Kleid den Mann macht!' In *Das Märchen vom falschen Prinzen* (1825), by Hauff, Labakan, a tailor of Alex-andria, with aspirations to gentility, steals the identity of a prince he meets; he is accepted by his long-lost 'father' but then detected and exposed; penitent, he sets up in business with magic materials and grows rich.

Closer still to the opening of *Kleider machen Leute* is Gaudy's *Aus dem Tagebuche eines wandernden Schneidergesellen* (1836). A tailor from Berlin is given a lift in a carriage, and rich meals at inns, by a German traveller whom from his appearance he takes for a nobleman—he wears 'einen dunkelblauen Carbonari-Mantel mit schwarzem Sammtkragen'. Gaudy's story seems to be the immediate source of *Der Schneidergeselle welcher den Herrn spielt*, published in the *Bündner Kalender* for 1847. We know that Keller contributed a story to this alman-ach, and some critics have assigned him this one. It seems more likely, however, that Keller's contribution was *Die misslungene*

Vergiftung, which is signed 'K', and that *Der Schneidergeselle* is the work of the editor, Friedrich Wassali. In it, a Berlin tailor, wandering in search of work, is picked up by a coach after he has mended the coachman's trousers; he acquires notions of nobility which are quickly deflated by three fellow-journeymen. This story must, of course, have been familiar to Keller.

Parallels also occur in stories not concerned with tailors. In *Fürst Ganzgott und Sänger Halbgott* (1818), by Arnim, an opera singer escapes from an irate audience in the costume of his aristocratic rôle, is taken for a prince at an inn in Karlsbad and treated accordingly. In his *Reisejournal*, ii, 3 (1831), Immermann describes a similar mistake at an inn in Leipzig: he and his companion are taken for expected gentry and served a splendid meal:

> Es bestand aber — denn bei solcher Gelegenheit ziemt sich wol die epische Weitläuftigkeit — aus Bouillon, kalten Forellen, Gänseleberpastete, Salmi von Rebhühnern, Schnepfenbraten, eingemachten französischen Früchten und Ananas.

In Marryat's *Peter Simple*, Ch. xiv (1834)—Keller is known to have read the novel—William Chucks assumes the identity of his master, a lord, after his death at sea, runs up bills with an innkeeper, wins money at cards, is troubled by conscience and intends to escape, but is unmasked before he can do so. He is a natural gentleman, and reappears later in the novel as a Swedish count. Jakob Frey's *Das erfüllte Versprechen* (1862) concerns a young man who arrives in Bern, is taken for a nobleman because of his fine features and gentle manners, but proves to be a hairdresser who has been brought up with a young nobleman. The impostor theme also appears in

Demetrius and *Veit Warbeck* by Schiller, with whom Keller was much preoccupied during the 1859 Centenary.

The fateful carriage transporting the hero to his fortune also appears frequently in Romantic fiction, from Hoffmann's *Das Gelübde* (1817) to Hauff's *Mitteilungen aus den Memoiren des Satan* and *Der Mann im Mond* and Eichendorff's *Aus dem Leben eines Taugenichts* (all 1826).

Finally, the sleigh-party. Goethe's friend Horn, in *Dichtung und Wahreit*, Bk. vi (1812), recites a poem in alexandrines describing a lovers' triangle during an excursion by sleigh; and Immermann's *Die Epigonen*, iv, 10 (1836), brings together the tailor and sleigh motifs.

It is neither possible nor essential to discover exactly which of these went to the making of *Kleider machen Leute*, consciously or otherwise, though we know that Keller was familiar with most of them. The important point is the extent to which his story, ostensibly drawn from life, links up with literary tradition and especially with Romantic writing. Must we, then, agree with Fontane that Keller 'ist au fond ein Märchen-erzähler', and see *Kleider machen Leute* as one more variant of the fairy-story themes of 'tailor makes fortune' and 'swineherd marries princess'?

The tone and treatment of the story make this view unten-able. Strapinksi has to overcome his longing for Utopia, abandon his impulse to 'solve' all problems by moving on from them, throw off the phantasy life of the Polish count. These undirected yearnings are ironized by the narrator, just as the Polish folk-song, the Romantic cult of national senti-ment, is ironized both through the tenor of the song itself ('Und Kathinka, dieses Saumensch . . .') and through

Nettchen's exaggerated response to it (Wüst detects an echo of Hauff's irony directed at uncritical enthusiasm for things Polish). All these fancies drop away: 'Keine Romane mehr!' Must we, then, see the *Novelle* as anti-Romantic?

The concluding section shows that this view is also incomplete. At the close, the narrator says of Strapinski: 'Dabei wurde er rund und stattlich und sah beinah gar nicht mehr träumerisch aus . . .' With 'beinah', Keller hints the assimilation of the irrational into the burgher world. In the Romantic stories, Tieck's *Abraham Tonelli* for example, the tailor makes good through a pure whim of fate. In Hauff's *Märchen von dem falschen Prinzen*, Labakan earns his fortune by repentance and endeavour, but the means of its achievement—a self-operating needle and cloth—are magical. In Strapinski's reinstatement, no magic as such is involved. Yet the resemblance between Nettchen and Wenzel's childhood friend is something magical, if by magic we mean the unexplained:

> Die allezeit etwas kokette Mutter Natur hatte hier eines ihrer Geheimnisse angewendet, um den schwierigen Handel zu Ende zu führen.

We are back at Auerbach's 'realistische Dichtung'. In his view of life, Keller brings together the imaginative reach of the Romantic individualist and the cautious consolidation of the Biedermeier burgher, just as in his creative technique he combines particular and universal in a symbolic whole.

Select Bibliography

A. TEXTS

Die Leute von Seldwyla, 2nd ed., Stuttgart, 1874, 4 vols. (the first edition of *Kleider machen Leute*, III, 7–83).

Sämtliche Werke, ed. Jonas Fränkel, Erlenbach-Zürich & München, VIII (= *Die Leute von Seldwyla*, II), 2nd ed., 1927 (the critical edition of *Kleider machen Leute*, pp. 5–69).

Kleider machen Leute, ed. Marcus Bachman Lambert, Boston &c., 1900, ix + 140 pp; new ed., London, [1902], reprinted 1955.

Gesammelte Briefe, ed. Carl Helbling, Bern, 1950–54, 4 vols.

B. STUDIES OF 'KLEIDER MACHEN LEUTE'

Paul Wüst, 'Entstehung und Aufbau von Gottfried Kellers Seldwyler Novelle "Kleider machen Leute"', *Mitteilungen der Literarhistorischen Gesellschaft Bonn*, IX, 1914, 77–142.

Schattkowsky, 'Gottfried Keller, *Kleider machen Leute*: Eine Einführung', *Pädagogisches Magazin, Beilage zum Archiv für Volksschullehrer*, XXXIV, 1931, 749–59.

E. Hoffmann-Krayer, 'Langbeins Novelle "Die schwarze Spinne" bei Gotthelf und Keller', *Sonntagsblatt der Basler Nachrichten*, 18 Oct. 1936.

Margarete Rothbarth, 'Das Urbild Strapinskis in "Kleider machen Leute"', *Neue Zürcher Zeitung*, 22 Nov. 1942.

Stuart Atkins, 'Vestis Virum Reddit (Gottfried Keller's "Kleider machen Leute")', *Monatshefte für den deutschen Unterricht*, XXXVI, 1944, 95–102.

John Hennig, 'A Note on Immermann's Influence on Keller', *Modern Language Review*, XLV, 1950, 519–23.

Mathilde Eppmann, 'Gottfried Keller: "Kleider machen Leute" (Versuch einer Stilbetrachtung)', *Deutschunterricht*, Stuttgart, [VI], 1953, no. 1, pp. 108–11.

Joachim Ziesenitz, 'Die Novelle im Unterricht', *Unsere Schule*, X, 1955, 410–17

Joachim Ziesenitz, 'Kleider machen Leute: Stoffquellen und Entstehungszeit', *Unsere Schule*, X, 1955, 417–20.

Joachim Ziesenitz, 'Die Menschen um Strapinski', *Unsere Schule*, X, 1955, 420–3.

Benno von Wiese, 'Gottfried Keller — Kleider machen Leute', in *Die deutsche Novelle von Goethe bis Kafka: Interpretationen*, Düsseldorf, 1956, pp. 238–49.

C. GENERAL CRITICISM

Charles C. Zippermann, *Gottfried Keller Bibliographie 1844–1934*, Zürich &c., 1935, [iv] + 227 pp.

Wolfgang Preisendanz, 'Die Keller-Forschung der Jahre 1939–1957', *Germanisch-Romanische Monatsschrift*, XXXIX, 1958, 144–78.

Berthold Auerbach, 'Gottfried Keller von Zürich', *Allgemeine Zeitung*, *Beilage*, 17 Apr. 1856.

Fernand Baldensperger, *Gottfried Keller: Sa Vie et ses Œuvres*, Paris, 1899, iii + v + 509 pp.

Albert Köster, *Gottfried Keller. Sieben Vorlesungen*, 1900; 4th ed., Leipzig, 1923, v + 154 pp.

Ricarda Huch, *Gottfried Keller* (= Die Dichtung, 9), Berlin & Leipzig, [1904], 100 pp; new ed. (= Insel-Bücherei, 113), Leipzig, [1914], 60 pp.

Emil Ermatinger, *Gottfried Kellers Leben*, 1915; 8th ed., Zürich, 1950, 640 pp.

Eduard Hitschmann, *Gottfried Keller: Psychoanalyse des Dichters* (= Internationale Psychoanalytische Bibliothek, 7), Leipzig &c., 1919, 125 pp.

Adam Lewak (Ed.), *Gottfried Keller und der polnische Freiheitskampf vom Jahre 1863/64*, Zürich &c., 1927, 156 pp.

Edgar Neis, *Romantik und Realismus in Gottfried Kellers Prosawerken* (= Germanische Studien, 85), Berlin, 1930, 101 pp.

Thomas Roffler, *Gottfried Keller: Ein Bildnis*, Frauenfeld & Leipzig, 1931, 222 pp.

Hildegard Demeter, *Gottfried Kellers Humor* (= Germanische Studien, 201), Berlin, 1938, 132 pp.

O. S. Fleissner, 'Bilder und Gleichnisse in Gottfried Kellers Prosawerken', *Publications of the Modern Language Association of America*, LV, 1940, 484–510.

Georg Lukács, *Gottfried Keller*, Berlin, 1946, 136 pp.

Hermann Boeschenstein, *Gottfried Keller: Grundzüge seines Lebens und Werkes*, Bern, 1948, 178 pp.

Alfred Zäch (Ed.), *Gottfried Keller im Spiegel seiner Zeit*, Zürich, 1952, [vi] + 267 pp.

Paula Ritzler, 'Das Aussergewöhnliche und das Bestehende in Gottfried Kellers Novellen', *Deutsche Vierteljahrsschrift für Literaturwissenschaft und Geistesgeschichte*, XXVIII, 1954, 373–83.

Edwin Keppel Bennet, *A History of the German Novelle from Goethe to Thomas Mann*, Cambridge, 1934, xiii + 296 pp., reprinted 1949.

Johannes Klein, *Geschichte der deutschen Novelle von Goethe bis zur Gegenwart*, Wiesbaden, 1954, xiv + 527 pp; 3rd ed., 1956, xviii + 614 pp.